PANKAJ'S NOTES FOR HAPPINESS

NOTES ON KINDNESS,
REGRET, LIFE &
EVERYTHING ELSE.

PANKAJ UPADHYAY

PREFACE

People have always said that treating people with kindness will make the world a better place. We have been taught it's the norm, but how many times are we actually kind to people, how many times have you helped a stranger on the road, or you've helped your colleagues in the office? How many times have you been nice to someone?

And especially when the person you've been kind to takes advantage of you? Do you still continue being kind? Is kindness now a concept that people just say for the sake of it? Is anyone you know truly kind? I'm sure there would be several examples coming to your mind. But are they kind 100% of the time? Do you know that give money to everyone to everyone who asks for it? I'm sure the answer is no, so what decided who to help and who to avoid? Life is complex and so are the situations. Not every situation needs to be handled with kindness.

This is not a book written by a psychologist or psychiatrist or even someone who has white hair. I'm 28, an entrepreneur, traveler, and a guy who's trying every day to survive in the complex world. I've realized that everyone is suffering, everyone has pain they are avoiding. It's not as simple as it seems. It's not easy to be kind and then be betrayed again and again.

There's a cancer spreading among all of us in the form of mental health, everyone is broken- some might accept it and some might say it's all hoax. And you just need to push through. You can always choose to be kind but what if your trust has been betrayed? You gave someone money because they said their kids are hungry but you see them using money for drinks. Or an employee who asked for a day off because she was sick but you see them having fun at concerts. There are just so many situations and I'm sure you might have thought of a situation in your mind as well.

Nature is kind but it also has anger, it also destructs. There's so much nature can take and it overpowers at times and results in the destruction of life as we know it on Earth.

There are mountains behind mountains but you can only see them if the clouds covering the peak are blown away by the air. You might not know what exists and what's real because we have a myopic view of the situation.

Kindness is a choice and you can choose when not to be kind. Being betrayed has consequences, it leads to deterioration in mental health. It leads to being in situations where you start being ruthless and mean to people without reason because it comes from your past and they have no idea where it's coming from.

As entrepreneurs, we have always wanted to change the world but how would we change the world if we ourselves are mentally sick? We are taking decisions with anxiety, and we want to change the world. Are we sure that it's the best decision we could have taken when we are suffering from anxiety? Don't we need to make sure to get better ourselves?

To,

Everyone who's suffering and looking for peace in life.

INTRODUCTION

There's a lot of anxiety in our daily life and they way I tackled it was to leave the city life and travel to different parts of India. I was in Macloedganj and met some amazing people with their own stories and struggles. I wasn't alone and I also knew a lot of people are looking for hope and happiness. Most of them had money but no one was really happy. And if money is not the root cause of happiness what is?

We usually relate being rich as being happy but that's generally not the case. So what are the truths to life that we need to understand to actually be happy and lead a life in which we can help a lot of people and not being broken and sick inside. This is a book with random notes, some might be relatable and some might just be weird. Iit's my journey to look inside, I always write when I'm anxious and this is what came out of it. It might not make sense to a lot of people but I hope for some of you it does and you also start taking care of yourself and not just a number you have made in your head.

You become a beacon of hope to someone and enlighten their life with happines.

INDEX

1. Being kind is a choice.
2. You don't always have to be kind. Saying no and prioritizing yourself is your choice.
3. Being selfish is not wrong. The better you're better you can help the world.
4. Being betrayed is usual.
5. Sometimes anger is useful. You don't have to be neutral.
6. In business, separate personal life from professional. Easier said than done, but if you can- you will be able to grow exponentially.
7. Life sucks, we suck, our friend sucks- no one is great and everyone is.
8. Mental health is a priority.
9. Choose YOU.

10. It's okay to not help everyone. You're not a god.

11. The situation changes so be ready for it.

12. Being kind is not a weakness if you're okay with consequences and results or lack of it.

13. You will not get a medal to be kind.

14. Kindness can lead to worse mental health so use it well and use it where you need it.

15. Nature is kind but also can be extremely deadly.

16. People can be kind only in certain situations.

17. Not everyone will treat you with kindness.

18. Life is a crazy place, do not try to think what everyone else is thinking.

19. It's complex, you won't be able to understand why someone is being mean to you so don't think about it.

20. People are suffering, don't add on it.

21. Be kind when you can.

22. Don't be kind when it's related to your mental peace.

23. Birds prey on birds if they see an opening, don't give other people that opening.

24. Good karma always helps but you can choose to do good with people who actually need it.

25. Breathe in and breathe out. Don't take breaths from someone else's life and make it hard for them.

26. Plant a tree, and give it life. Be kind and help it grow.

27. Pay for someone's education, and make a change in their life. Help them grow.

28. Walk, and use less fuel so nature doesn't get angry and stop being kind to us.

29. Talk to people, listen to their pain. Don't give advice, you don't know them.

30. Wait for the clouds to clear up to see the mountain behind the mountain and let the picture clear up before your eyes.

31. If the dog is barking, you don't have to bark with them. But don't take your eyes off them at least for a bit.

32. People have time to waste, don't spend it with them.

33. Help elderly people. It's good.

34. You will regret. Accept that.

35. Regret is not always bad. Not every moment needs to be acted upon.

36. Don't have regrets if you can act upon it.

37. Don't shed tears because of regret.

38. Take action when you realize you suck and have regrets.

39. Don't be always nice and then regret it later. Say no.

40. Love people, say nice things.

41. Say no, it's your choice.

42. Being light in darkness is a choice, you can be part of darkness and take it easy. Not everyone is meant to be a light.

43. Nature is powerful, don't mess with it.

44. Regret is powerful make sure you only do it once.

45. You don't have to change the world, it's okay if you're living in it.

46. Smiling is not for everyone, it's okay if you don't smile.

47. That person's life sucks too, if they made your life hell.

48. Fall in love.

49. Don't regret the regret.

50. Take your time, there's a way.

51. If you lose, you're not losing.

52. Don't chase that person, it's not leading anywhere.

53. Talk to strangers, you will like it.

54. Listen always.

55. Stop and communicate.

56. Being loud is a choice, use it aptly.

57. Walk more, it helps.

58. Laugh even if it hurts and hurts really bad.

59. Sleep in a bed that doesn't hurt your back and neck.

60. Hug people, it's nice.

61. Don't be nice to everyone. Not everyone deserves it.

62. A game is being played with defined roles, it's okay if your life is a template and decided.

63. You don't have to fight, you can survive by pretending to be dead.

64. You're not crazy, you're just being nice.

65. The wind is nice, feel it.

66. Dance to the rhythm of nature, it's already in you.

67. Take care of the people, you can do it.

68. You can run, if you don't want to fight it.

69. Decide when you want to face it or don't. It's your choice.

70. Life will suck, enjoy it.

71. Light is enlightening you don't have to be inspired by them.

72. Be you, be dull, be stupid. Everything is okay.

73. Back To Basics

74. We have the tools, basic life is a great life.

75. Vibes with basic home are a vibe you need.

76. It's all in you.

77. Being in the moment is the hardest task you will ever achieve.

78. Rainy nights have powerful sounds.

79. Lightning is nature's way to show its might.

80. Be with nature, don't destroy it.

81. Mountains are pretty wild, be wild.

82. Be in harmony with yourself.

83. One step at a time, that's all you have to do.

84. You can't walk straight on a mountain. Start loving the curves.

85. Sitting on a desk and facing a view, sit on the opposite desk and you will see a different world.

86. Music helps you focus.

87. People are complex, you don't have to understand them.

88. If you're in the mountains, don't expect it to be clear all the time.

89. People are beautiful, say hello.

90. If it's quiet, don't be loud.

91. Listen to the birds, they communicate to all the different species of birds.

92. If it's cold, experience it.

93. Every moment in the world is pretty and beautiful for someone.

94. Beliefs are strong, learn how to use them.

95. Stretch your body, it does wonders.

96. Listen to the sound of water, it heals.

97. Dogs are caring, love them.

98. Every place has a vibe, feel it.

99. Every organism on the Earth is communicating, observe it.

100. Eat light, and feel better.

101. Talk to people but not all.

102. Sharing is powerful but not with everyone.

103. A home with a TV is great but a home with peace is greater.

104. Love is great, experience it.

105. Clear is not clarity.

106. Patience is good if your eyes are concentrated on your goal.

107. Work is beautiful if you enjoy it.

108. Raindrops leave their mark, you just see it on water.

109. Look up. Right now.

110. Feeling warm and safe in winter and rain is not a blessing.

111. Focus is when you cut a tree because you know that's how you feed your family.

112. That primal feeling of running in a jungle, your mind will take you there.

113. Your past life you were what you think.

114. An Axe is more powerful than a sword. You can feed people with it.

115. A good hunt is when you can have people to eat with.

116. You can understand anyone, you just need to be patient and spend time.

117. There's a universal language being spoken in the world, you will experience it.

118. Feel the chill, it keeps you on your toes.

119. Sit straight, it's good for your back.

120. Enjoy the sun but do know it can burn you too.

121. Feel the vibration in your soul.

122. Whatever makes you feel better it's art.

123. Walk where you're going.

124. Lights flicker, you just don't see it when you're close to them.

125. What's your pain, ask a mother who couldn't push.

126. You won't know who you're going to meet the next moment, be ready for it.

127. You can't like everyone nor you will be liked by everyone, deal with it.

128. Being humble is attractive.

129. Pain leads to a new beautiful path.

130. Being cold has its perks, you can hold someone's hand.

131. Have water, it's healthy.

132. Sound of rain, it's pretty.

133. Life is a negotiation, either you negotiating with yourself, others, or nature. And in the negotiation nature will always win.

134. When things are not in your control that's when you know how helpless you can get.

135. You can't be friends with everyone, so don't try.

136. When you don't wanna be liked by everyone you will be liked by people who you like.

137. Being at height has its cost.

138. Find the exact problem statement and start from there.

139. Write when you can.

140. Focus comes when you sit.

141. Being alone is not bad, being in a group and feeling alone is.

142. Crazy thing about life is that it's beautiful yet sucks, it's pretty brutal yet amazing.

143. The skyline merges with the cloud and makes the world feel small.

144. Don't try to get involved where you don't belong.

145. Give people a chance to come to you and if they don't, they are not meant for you.

146. You won't be a king to an estate but you can be a leader.

147. Risks are great, take them.

148. Learn when to step out of the rut and make new stories.

149. Travel more, you don't know what you will experience next.

150. There's a crazy thing going on in the world that people work for

money and then say they can't find happiness.

151. Be free, feel free. Don't own assets you don't need. Be minimal.

152. Don't be a slave to technology.

153. There's a war going on, either you can be a pawn or open your eyes and not participate in it.

154. There's a time when you have to say enough and then deal with it.

155. Wars can't be won without a fight.

156. You will be attracted to people, acting on it or not is your choice.

157. Every decision you make will lead your life in a different direction and you're making hundreds or thousands of choices daily without thought and that's where you realize how your past defines you and how you're different from others.

158. There's something lovely about seeing people in love, it gives you hope but there's also something great about seeing a couple fighting but also making up and compromising.

159. You won't find a perfect person, there might be someone perfect for some period of time but as their choices change or they change that might not be something you find perfect now it's your choice, do you go looking in the world to find that perfect person again or do you stay with the person you know.

160. Work is always a part of life, but there's so much to it. Caring about people, helping people, loving your partner, your family and just loving the world. The world might not be a nice place but you can still pass through it smiling.

161. Leverage is powerful, it's really powerful in life and in business try learning how to take leverage.

162. Searching for meaning in life is not a day job or even a month job, it's a constant process. Meaning changes with time and the people you meet along with the situations in life.

163. Thinking about the worst situation makes you ready but you can also spiral out, so don't overthink.

164. Taking a break sometimes is required, it's not easy to make your mind quiet but practice it, it's peaceful.

165. Hope is the most powerful thing you can give to people. When all seems lost, giving hope has the most value.

166. Walk, it's good for your health.

167. The world will have people who will appreciate roses and people who will see that it grows on thorns.

168. There's so much in this world to see, always be learning. You don't know everything, listen to people.

169. Conflict resolution can only happen if the two parties are ready to listen. It requires skill to make them think they both won and it will only end if the outcome gets both of them what they require the most and it can be very different.

170. There's a game being played, can you see what role are you playing on the chessboard?

171. City life is a busy life.

172. Loving life is not easy, it gets tiresome but if you see it from a different perspective it will show you a completely other side.

173. Giving hope is powerful.

174. When you start working on things you should go ahead and do them.

175. The weather can change anytime, some might predict it but it's your choice to accept and get ready for it or leave it as it is.

176. You want things, things take attention. Attention takes happiness.

177. If you've hope today, it's a great day.

178. The universe is amazing, Feel it. The universe is always helping you, you just need to understand that it's supporting you.

179. Want to help people? Get better yourself.

180. When you move the world will revolve around you but you have to more.

EPILOGUE

I hope some of the words related to you, in the end happiness is something you've to work yourself.

Money is not happiness, things are not happiness. Happiness truly comes from sharing, it comes from inside. It comes when you're one with the nature and help people, help the environment, do a good deed. We always ask what do we get in return, you get good karma and a smile. And it helps in making the world a better place.

You don't have to listen to me, or others. You just have to look inside, do what feels honest and right to you. Leading a simple life is hard when you're surrounded by things and a narrative of your friends and family. You need to take the decision and prioritise yourself. You're amazing and important to the universe and nature. Utilise your full potential and be better yourself so you can help others and be one with the nature.

Printed by Libri Plureos GmbH in Hamburg, Germany